About the Author

Larry Burkett is committed to teaching God's people His principles for managing money. Unfortunately, money management is one area often neglected by Christians, and it is a major cause of conflict and disruption in both business and family life.

For more than two decades Larry has counseled and taught God's principles for finance across the country. As director of Christian Financial Concepts, Larry has counseled, conducted seminars, and written numerous books on the subject of maintaining control of the budget. In additon he is heard on more than 1000 radio outlets worldwide.

LARRY BURKETT

FINANCIAL FREEDOM

MOODY PRESS
CHICAGO

© 1991 by
CHRISTIAN FINANCIAL CONCEPTS

Compiled from material originally published by Christian Financial Concepts, Inc.

All Scripture quotations, unless noted otherwise, are from the *New American Standard Bible,* © 1960, 1962, 1963, 1968, 1971, 1972, 1973, 1975, and 1977 by The Lockman Foundation, and are used by permission.

ISBN: 0-8024-2604-2

3 5 7 9 10 8 6 4

Printed in the United States of America

Financial Freedom

TYPES OF BONDAGE

What is financial bondage? As we look at Scripture, it becomes obvious that it means excessive debts. If a debtor could not repay his obligations, the lender had the right to imprison him until he could pay back every cent. The lender then owned everything that had once belonged to the debtor—his wife, his family, all of his possessions.

PHYSICAL BONDAGE

The biblical perspective of bondage is expressed in Matthew 5:25-26: "Make friends quickly with your opponent at law while you are with him on the way, in order that your opponent may not deliver you to the judge, and the judge to the officer, and you be thrown into prison. Truly I say to you, you shall not come out of there, until you have paid up the last

5

cent." In the Bible financial bondage means physical bondage.

Such harsh treatment was meted out because failure to repay a debt was equated with dishonesty. Dishonesty was judged so strictly that usually when a thief was caught, his hand was cut off as a punishment for his crime. Someone who failed to repay an obligation was thrown into prison for the rest of his life or sold as a slave. Why? When one gave his word, he was expected to keep it. Anyone who failed to do so could not be trusted. Today society has become too sophisticated to incarcerate someone simply because of debts. Unfortunately a new punishment has supplanted the old one.

MENTAL BONDAGE

Physical bondage has been replaced by mental bondage. Every year thousands of families are destroyed because of financial bondage. Thousands, perhaps millions, of people encumber themselves with debts beyond their ability to repay. Credit cards have supplied the means to buy on impulse, allowing virtually anyone to encumber himself far beyond his ability to repay.

No Allowance for Avoiding Creditors

There may be legal remedies to avoid creditors, such as bankruptcy, but there are no scriptural remedies. "The wicked borrows and does not pay back, but the righteous is gracious and gives" (Psalm 37:21).

In worldly terms that principle does not seem logical. Many Christians even begin to doubt God, saying, "How will I live if they take everything?"

Thus we begin to seek ways to shelter possessions from legitimate creditors. But Christians cannot do that. We must accept the fact that God is in control and that He understands our needs and promises to provide them.

God's Promise

If we really trust God with everything that we have, He will satisfy all of our needs as He promised. "For all these things the nations of the world eagerly seek; but your Father knows that you need these things. But seek for His kingdom, and these things shall be added to you" (Luke 12:30-31).

God asked Abraham to sacrifice his most important possession—his son Isaac. Born of his old age, Isaac was Abraham's true love, and although Abraham was a wealthy man by worldly standards, nothing meant as much to him as Isaac.

But God asked Abraham to take his son up to the mountains and sacrifice him unto the Lord. He asked Abraham, as He asks us, to sacrifice everything for His name's sake. Abraham could have argued with God, but he did not. He knew that since God had given him a son in his old age, surely God could recover him from death.

So he packed up the mules, his servants, and Isaac and set out for the mountain. Having laid his son upon the altar, Abraham raised the knife.

At that point God stopped him, saying, "Abraham, I know that you are a true man, and you have your seed as abundant as the sand upon the shore. And I'll bless you beyond every nation on earth" (cf. Genesis 22:16-17).

Not only did Abraham love and trust God, but he bowed his will to God's judgment. Christians must accept this concept of total stewardship because when they transfer assets or file bankruptcy to avoid creditors or deal deceitfully with creditors, they block God's channel for help.

BONDAGE THROUGH WEALTH

Financial bondage can also exist through an abundance of money. Those who use their money totally for self-satisfaction or hoard it away for that elusive "rainy day" are just as financially bound in God's eyes as those in debt.

The accumulation of wealth and material pleasures of life can be an obsession that destroys a Christian's health and family, separates him from friends, and blocks God's will in his life. Everything and everybody can become objects to help him climb the ladder to success. Job 31:24-28 says,

> If I have put my confidence in gold, and called fine gold my trust, if I have gloated because my wealth was great, and because my hand had secured so much; if I have looked at the sun when it shone, or the moon going in splendor, and my heart became secretly enticed, and my hand threw a kiss from my mouth, that too would have been an iniquity calling for judgment, for I would have denied God above.

It is important for Christians to understand this truth. Many Christians have taken the very resource that God has provided for their peace and comfort and transformed it into something of pain and sorrow. There is nothing inherently evil in money itself—only in the preoccupation with and misuse of it.

SYMPTOMS OF BONDAGE

Many get sucked into bondage because they are addicted to acquiring possessions. We need to learn to recognize the symptoms of financial bondage.

OVERDUE BILLS

A Christian is in financial bondage when he experiences anxiety about overdue bills. Up to 80 percent of Christian families suffer from overspending or have suffered from it in the past. That is partly because most families have no plan for their finances and continue to borrow beyond their ability to repay.

If a Christian is shackled in this area, it is virtually impossible to be an effective witness for Jesus Christ. Frustration in the home life is reflected in the spiritual life. Proverbs 27:12 says, "A prudent man sees evil and hides himself, the naive proceed and pay the penalty." God says that a man who plans well foresees dangers and avoids them, but the foolish man rushes in, does whatever is convenient—and ends up paying the penalty later.

INVESTMENT WORRIES

Worrying over investments, savings, money, or assets also causes financial bondage and interferes with the Christian's spiritual life. As they begin to accumulate material goods (or worry about not accumulating them), many Christians carry over worry to other areas of their lives. They never enjoy their families because of their concern over investments or lack of investments.

If his investments generate worry, a Christian can be absolutely sure that he is not within God's will. "No one can serve two masters; for either he will hate the one and love the other, or he will hold to one and despise the other. You cannot serve God and mammon. For this reason I say to you, do not be anxious for your life, as to what you shall eat, or what you shall drink; nor for your body, as to what you shall put on. Is not life more than food, and the body than clothing?" (Matthew 6:24-25).

GET-RICH-QUICK ATTITUDE

This attitude is characterized by attempts to make money quickly with little applied effort. An investment is a get-rich-quick program if an individual must assume excessive debt, borrow the money to invest, or deal deceitfully with people.

Proverbs says that a man who wants to get rich fast will quickly fail. "A faithful man will abound with blessings, but he who makes haste to be rich will not go unpunished" (Proverbs 28:20). Money that may have taken years of effort to accumulate can be lost in days in a get-rich-quick program.

NO GAINFUL EMPLOYMENT

Financial bondage also exists when there is no desire for gainful employment. Paul says in 2 Thessalonians 3:10, "For even when we were with you, we used to give you this order: if anyone will not work, neither let him eat."

Unfortunately we have lost this perspective in society today. The government has assumed responsibility to support the deserving and the undeserving. Each of us must have a desire to work if we are to accomplish what God put us on this earth to do.

When someone wants assistance a Christian should ask himself, "Is he asking me to supply his needs, wants, or desires? Does this individual really have an internal commitment to work?" It is possible to hinder God's perfect plan in another's life by satisfying his or her requests.

Paul is a good example of the proper attitude here. He worked throughout his Christian life. But in his travels Paul found many Christians who had no desire to work. They relied on the brethren to take care of them. Paul admonished those people. He reminded the believers who worked that it wasn't their responsibility to support those who didn't. "Now we command you, brethren, in the name of our Lord Jesus Christ, that you keep aloof from every brother who leads an unruly life and not according to the tradition which you received from us" (2 Thessalonians 3:6).

DECEITFULNESS

A Christian is in financial bondage if he is dishonest in financial matters. Have you dealt honestly and openly with everyone? For instance, someone selling insurance or investments can easily shade the truth. That deceit will financially bind a Christian, destroying his peace and contentment.

Christian families must make a similar assessment. Bondage can occur, for instance, if a couple purchases an appliance on credit, knowing that they are already behind in their average monthly obligations. They are dealing deceitfully with the supplier.

Luke 16:10 relates God's attitude toward deceit: "He who is faithful in a very little thing is faithful also in much; and he who is unrighteous in a very little thing is unrighteous also in much." If we are not faithful in small things, we will not be faithful in large things. The amount is not important.

GREEDINESS

Financial bondage also results from greed, which is reflected when someone always wants the best or always wants more than he has. Someone who is never able to put others first, never able to accept a necessary loss, or always looking at what others have suffers from greed. A Christian who cannot put his own wants behind him to satisfy the needs of others is greedy. "For this you know with certainty, that no immoral or impure person or covetous man, who is an idolater, has an inheritance in the kingdom of Christ and God" (Ephesians 5:5). What is an idolator? One who puts material possessions before God.

The rich ruler of Luke 18 suffered from this malady. He put his money before God, and he could not give up that idol, even to follow Christ.

COVETOUSNESS

Financial bondage exists if a Christian looks at what others have and desires it. We call that "keeping up with the Joneses."

I often hear young couples talk about their start on the road to indebtedness. They simply followed the example of people who borrowed to get the things they wanted—furniture, new cars, and televisions.

It's too bad they can't look inside the Joneses' house. They need to see the strife when the paycheck comes and there's not enough to satisfy all the creditors. Or the anxiety when a notice comes from a collection agency taking them to court.

Covetousness should not characterize the Christian. Set your goals and standards based on God's conviction—not on what others possess. Peace and contentment are worth any price.

FAMILY NEEDS UNMET

A Christian is in financial bondage if his family's needs cannot be met because of his past buying habits. The reasons for unmet needs can be many: a Christian may refuse gainful employment; he may be shackled with debts to the point that creditors take necessary family funds; the standard of living may allow luxuries to deprive the family of needs. Many Christians live far beyond their means and sacrifice basic necessities such as medical or dental care to do so.

The symptoms of financial bondage are almost inexhaustible, but they are all related to a common attitude—irresponsibility. There is a definite difference between a Christian who is financially bound because of irresponsibility and one who cannot meet family needs because of circumstances such as medical bills, injury, illness, or other unforeseeable events. In those instances it is the responsibility of other Christians to help satisfy the family needs.

The financial bondage I am talking about here occurs because of bad habits and an unwillingness to meet the needs of their families. Paul says in 1 Timothy 5:8, "But if any one does not provide for his own, and especially for those in his household, he has denied the faith, and is worse than an unbeliever."

UNMET CHRISTIAN NEEDS

Unfortunately, unmet needs in the church is the norm in today's Christianity. But it is the responsibility of each Christian to supply the needs of others who cannot do so for themselves.

James 2:15-16 states, "If a brother or sister is without clothing and in need of daily food, and one of you says to them, 'Go in peace, be warmed and be filled,' and yet you do not give them what is necessary for their body, what use is that?"

Harry Truman made a famous statement about the presidency, "The buck stops here," and the same is true for each Christian. If we see a brother or sister in need, and we close our hearts to that need, what kind of love is that? Of course, God will not lay every need on every Christian's heart, but He does lay on our hearts specific needs that we are to meet.

OVERCOMMITMENT TO WORK

A life that is devoted to business pursuits to the exclusion of all else is a life of bondage. Not only are many Christians worried and frustrated about investments, but their lives are dominated by work; everywhere they go their work follows them, and every discussion is centered on their business. But God's plan for work is to excel, not exceed.

MONEY ENTANGLEMENTS

God says a Christian is in financial bondage when his money entanglements reduce his Christian effectiveness. Entanglements differ from overcommitment to work in that they stem from a mishandling of finances, perhaps even deceitfulness. It is a case of having "too many irons in the fire."

Someone trapped by entanglements is so stretched that he has to continually apply Band-Aids to his financial ventures. Often someone in this situation has dealt with so many people unfairly that he can no longer be an effective witness for Christ, and many times he has also involved other friends in his ventures.

Remember the parable of the sower? Some of the seed fell among the thorns, which were the pressures and riches of life. As these grew up, they choked out God's Word. A Christian can understand God's Word and be willing to obey it, but the pressures and riches of life can choke it out so that he or she no longer responds.

FINANCIAL UNFAIRNESS

God says a Christian is in financial bondage if he deals unfairly with others. He promotes his own interests to the detriment of others. A classic example is the Christian who discovers someone in need and pressures the needy person to accept a poor offer or forces him to borrow.

People often use this tactic with new widows. Widows are besieged by "Christian" wolves who attempt to sell them things they don't need or

19

encourage them to make investments when they are vulnerable.

Many people use religious contacts as a means to solicit business—approaching others at church and applying pressure because of Christian involvement. Young couples often over-buy life insurance from an older individual who is a church leader.

But God warns those with this attitude, "He who increases his wealth by interest and usury, gathers it for him who is gracious to the poor" (Proverbs 28:8). Such an individual is never able to deny himself a material desire but instead satisfies his every whim.

God promises to satisfy every *need* that we have, not every desire. The self-indulgent can be identified by one or more of the following signs:

1. Purchasing without regard for utility
2. Living a lifestyle characterized by lavishness
3. Consistently trading cars and appliances for newer models
4. Filling closet after closet with clothes that are seldom or never used
5. Spending money frivolously on any "sale" item

LACK OF COMMITMENT TO GOD'S WORK

A Christian is in financial bondage if he or she has no financial commitment to God's work. This principle is basic to Christian financial management. "Honor the Lord from your wealth, and from the first of all your produce; so your barns will be filled with plenty, and your vats will overflow with new wine" (Proverbs 3:9-10). It is only by honoring the Lord from the first part of our income that God can take control. We are stewards; God is the owner. The tithe that we give to God is a testimony of His ownership. (The booklet titled *Giving and Tithing* also discusses this subject.)

FINANCIAL SUPERIORITY

Someone who has wealth should think of it not as a right but as a responsibility. There should be no attitude of financial superiority within the Body of Christ. According to God's plan, he who has much should share it with those who have little. But many Christians and Christian organizations cater to wealthy individuals, and many wealthy Christians demand special attention.

FINANCIAL RESENTMENT

The converse of superiority is resentment because of God's provision, thinking God has not given what an individual thinks he or she deserves. Not only does that person covet what others have, but he also resents God for his station in life.

Assess any feelings of resentment in relation to need rather than desire. We live better than 98 percent of the rest of the population on earth.

It is easy to adjust to large homes, two cars, automatic washers and dryers, refrigerators, and air conditioners and then to begin to feel resentful because of all the things other people have. In a time of plenty many want to adjust to lavishness.

Do you believe that everything works together to accomplish God's will for your life? Consider John 6:27: "Do not work for the food which perishes, but for the food which endures to eternal life, which the Son of Man shall give to you, for on Him the Father, even God, has set His seal." Be fearful of resentful feelings lest you begin to resent even God.

MISUNDERSTANDING GOD'S PROVISION

Financial bondage can develop not only from a lack of money or overspending but also from an abundance of money or from misunderstanding why God gives it to us.

Adjusting our spending level to exceed our income results in financial bondage, and borrowing is the most common way into bondage. Every Christian must understand God's attitude toward debt. The Bible discusses little about what we buy with borrowed money but describes in depth our requirement to repay.

Common sense should tell us not to borrow for depreciating assets. They are usually worth less than the amount we borrow and may well fall into what God calls surety. Surety is putting yourself up as a guarantor for material assets. But the economy determines whether a particular item is depreciating or appreciating.

There is a range of possible responses a Christian may have regarding borrowing. One extreme is expressed in Romans 13:8, "Owe nothing to anyone except to love one another; for he who loves his neighbor has fulfilled the law." Here God describes borrowing in terms of owing no man.

I know personally that there is no greater sense of freedom than to owe no man any financial obligation.

The other end of the range is found in Psalm 37:21, "The wicked borrows and does not pay back, but the righteous is gracious and gives." God requires repayment of every obligation. Every Christian must operate between those two points.

Debt and Credit

Nothing in the area of finances has so dominated or influenced the direction of our society during the last fifty years as debt. It's amazing when you consider that only a generation ago credit cards were unknown, car loans were a rarity, and mortgages were for GIs who were getting their starter homes. No one in our fathers' or grandfathers' generations would have believed that any banker would be so foolish as to lend a teenager money to go to college. Instead their counsel was, "Get a job."

Today it is not unusual for a young couple to owe nearly $100,000 within the first two years of marriage. A profile of a young couple's debt often reveals their financial training—or lack of it—including a home mortgage of approximately $65,000, college loans (his and hers) of $20,000, and car loans (his and hers) of $13,000. Often the list extends even further to include consolidation loans, finance company loans, and parental loans.

Wise Christians would say we're supposed to take our direction from God's Word, not from the world. So the logical response would be to observe what the church is doing and use that as our guide. However, the average American church is as deeply in debt as the average American business—and with about the same rate of delinquent payments and bankruptcies.

The only reliable source of wisdom, then, is the Word of God itself. Only by going back to the true source of wisdom can we possibly hope to find the right balance today. God's Word tells us that His plan for us is to be debt-free. And even better, we should be lenders rather than borrowers. Read Deuteronomy 28:12: "The Lord will open for you His good storehouse, the heavens, to give rain to your land in its season and to bless all the work of your hand; and you shall lend to many nations, but you shall not borrow."

I believe that debt-free living is still God's plan for us today. The blessings of becoming debt-free go far beyond the financial area. They extend to the spiritual and marital realms. No one who is financially bound can be spiritually free. The problems will certainly spill over into your prayer and study time. And the effects of financial bondage on a marriage relationship are measurable in the statistics of failed marriages. Approximately 50 percent of all first marriages fail, and "finances" are listed as the leading cause of divorce by a factor of four to one.

What about the individual who is already in debt? What can he or she do to break out of that cycle? How much debt and credit can a family practically handle? Is there a balance? The purpose of this booklet is to address those questions, but I would like to state the conclusion now: *Anyone can become debt-free and stay that way, given the desire, discipline, and time.*

WHAT IS DEBT?

Most simply put, a debt is something that is owed. The Bible does not prohibit a person from borrowing, but it does warn against surety, or the taking on a debt without an absolutely sure way to repay it. Therefore, for the purposes of this booklet let's define debt as "a condition that exists when a loan commitment is not met, or inadequate collateral is pledged to unconditionally satisfy a loan agreement." Debt exists when any of the following conditions are true:

1. Payment is past due for money, goods, or services that have been purchased.
2. The total value of unsecured liabilities exceeds total assets. In other words, if you had to cash out at any time, there would be a negative balance on your account.
3. Anxiety is produced over financial responsibility, and the family's basic needs are not met because of past or present buying practices.

Although the terms *debt* and *credit* are often used interchangeably in our society, they are definitely not the same. Credit is "the establishment of a mutual trust relationship between a lender and a borrower (or potential borrower)."

How Does a Person Establish Credit?

Many young people get into trouble with credit because they are desperate to establish credit and it is easy to qualify for more credit than they can manage.

The best way to establish credit is to borrow against an acceptable asset. For example, if you have saved $1,000 and want to borrow the same amount, almost any bank will lend you $1,000 using the savings as collateral. Usually the lender will charge from 1 to 2 percent more for the loan than the prevailing savings rate. So in essence it costs about 2 percent interest to establish a good credit history. For a one-year loan of $1,000, the net cost would be approximately $20.

Then, by using the bank as a credit reference, almost anyone can qualify for a major credit card, although the credit limit would normally be the minimum amount. I am not advocating that everyone should rush out and obtain a credit card, but the point is that credit is relatively simple to establish if you have already acquired the discipline of saving.

Having someone (a relative or friend) cosign for a loan is a common way to establish credit, but it is also a major form of surety and as such should be avoided. "Do not be among those who give pledges, among those who become sureties for debts" (Proverbs 22:26).

DANGER OF BORROWING

Why are Christians trapped by borrowing? Because they have violated one or more of the scriptural principles God has laid down, particularly those relating to financial bondage. Proverbs 22:7 says, "The rich rules over the poor, and the borrower becomes the lender's slave." God says that when someone borrows, he becomes a servant of the lender; the lender becomes an authority over the borrower. This should clearly define God's attitude about borrowing from secular sources to do His work.

Christians can get into financial bondage in one of two ways.

CREDIT BONDAGE

The most common type of bondage is excessive use of credit. Many individuals today think the credit card companies will not allow them to borrow beyond their ability to repay, but such is not the case. The average credit card company in the United States allows an individual to borrow 250 percent more than he can conceivably repay.

Delinquent accounts are generally regulated by statutes favoring the creditor, meaning that delinquent debts fall under a different set of rules. Those rules allow the creditors to charge more interest for debts in delinquency than they can for accounts that are current.

DEBT

The scriptural definition of a debt is the inability to meet agreed-upon obligations. When a person buys something on credit, that is not necessarily a debt; it is a contract. But when the terms of that contract are violated, scriptural debt occurs.

The fact that someone is in debt is the result of misunderstanding or disobeying God's principles. "And He said to them, 'Beware, and be on your guard against every form of greed; for not even when one has an abundance does his life consist of his possessions'" (Luke 12:15). When a Christian continues to borrow without the means to repay, his attitude falls into the category of deceit and greed.

Many Christians are shackled by excessive debts, and misuse of finances has ruined their spiritual lives. They are no longer able to minister to people as God directs; they feel encumbered and are timid in speaking about Christ. They are also defeated in their homes, harassed by their spouses, and frustrated or intimidated by creditors.

Proverbs 21:17 says, "He who loves pleasure will become a poor man; he who loves wine and oil will not become rich." One who is never willing to sacrifice or deny his impulses but constantly seeks to indulge his whimsical desires will always be in bondage. Until a Christian brings his debts under control according to God's plan, he will not realize peace. Remember, God is concerned with our attitude; He will begin to work in a Christian's finances, regardless of past actions, as soon as his or her attitude is correct.

WHAT DOES THE BIBLE SAY ABOUT BORROWING?

The Bible gives some principles concerning borrowing, although it must be remembered that they are principles, not laws. A principle is an instruction from the Lord to help guide our decisions. A law is an absolute. Negative consequences may result from ignoring a principle, but direct punishment is the likely consequence of ignoring a God-given law.

Principles are given to keep us clearly within God's path so that we can experience His blessings. To ignore them puts us in a constant state of jeopardy in which Satan can cause us to stumble at any time.

The principle of borrowing in Scripture is that it is better not to go surety on a loan. "A man lacking in sense pledges, and becomes surety in the presence of his neighbor" (Proverbs 17:18). Again, surety means that you take on an obligation to pay without a specific way to pay it.

The law of borrowing in Scripture is that it is a sin to borrow and not repay. "The wicked borrows and does not pay back, but the righteous is gracious and gives" (Psalm 37:21). The assumption in the verse is that the wicked person can repay but will not, as opposed to an individual who wants to repay but cannot.

Some teach that Romans 13:8 is a scriptural injunction (law) against all forms of borrowing. In this verse Paul says, "Owe nothing to anyone except to love one another; for he who loves his neighbor has fulfilled the law." However, I believe that in the context Paul is summing up the prescribed duty for all men to pay their taxes and respect government officials, not giving a new teaching on the subject of borrowing.

To put it simply, although the Bible does not prohibit borrowing, it certainly does not recommend it.

How Can a Person Borrow and Not Become Surety?

Remember that surety is taking on an obligation without an absolutely certain way to repay. For example, suppose you want to buy a car costing $10,000. You put $2,000 down and sign a note for $8,000, pledging the car as collateral and guaranteeing the note by signing a deficiency agreement. You have become surety because if you are not able to make the payments and default on the loan, the car is repossessed, sold (usually at a loss), and you are required to make up the difference (deficiency).

If, on the other hand, you don't sign a deficiency agreement and don't guarantee the contract beyond the car as total collateral, you would not be surety. However, you would find that you also would not have a car because the lender won't make the loan under those conditions. Of course, if you have a substantially larger down payment (and thus a smaller loan), you could conceivably put the car as total collateral (since its sale would fully cover the deficiency) and solve the problem of surety. If you could not pay the note, all you would have to do is give back the collateral and you would be released from the note—free and clear.

COMMON ATTITUDES THAT LEAD TO DEBT

IGNORANCE

Many of us simply were never trained, either formally or by example, to manage our money. Our society is no help—its philosophy is spend, spend, spend. If you can't afford it, get it anyway because you deserve it. That type of attitude leads to indulgence.

INDULGENCE

We tend to think we need everything *now*. Somehow it has become our "right" to have at least two new cars, a nice home, exciting vacations, and so on. The whole concept of starting out small and patiently improving our lifestyle one step at a time has certainly flown out the window.

POOR PLANNING

No matter how noble our intentions may be, a person without a plan that gauges income versus expenditures is on the road to debt and financial troubles.

How to Get Out of Debt

Proverbs 22:3 says, "The prudent sees the evil and hides himself, but the naive go on, and are punished for it." Again, anyone can become debt-free and stay that way, given the desire, discipline, and time. Proverbs 10:22 says, "It is the blessing of the Lord that makes rich, and He adds no sorrow to it." If you have a lot of debt and a get-rich-quick mentality, you will bring depression into your family. You need to commit to a renewed relationship with the Lord and understand that God has everything under His control. Here are some important steps to take to get out of debt and stay out.

STOP ANY FORM OF BORROWING

Do not borrow anything—and that includes using your credit cards. Here is a recipe for getting out of debt: Preheat your oven to 425 degrees, grease a cookie pan, toss your credit cards on it, and bake ten minutes or until done. Consumer credit is the most common source of indebtedness for Americans, and the sooner you stop borrowing, the sooner you will get out of debt.

DEVELOP A BUDGET

A budget is a plan for managing money in your home. If you are in debt, it will need to be a fairly restrictive budget for at least a year, maybe more. A good place to start is to obtain *A Guide to Family Budgeting* or *Personal Finances* from your local bookstore.

WORK OUT A PAY-BACK PLAN

Work out a plan with your creditors to pay your debts. Most creditors are more than willing to work with people who honestly want to repay them.

LEARN TO TRUST GOD

Start to trust God for the things you truly need but can't afford. Remember, God may not want you to have an item that you thought you needed but really could do without.

EXERCISE SELF-DISCIPLINE

Curb your impulse to buy. If you haven't budgeted for it, don't buy it.

SEEK COUNSEL

Many of us need assistance with establishing and maintaining a budget and working with creditors. Christian Financial Concepts operates a referral counselor network to link families in need of financial counsel with trained volunteer counselors in their local area.

In summary, when considering the subject of debt and credit, Christians should base their decisions upon the principles of God's Word—not the world's conventional "wisdom."

ANSWERS TO QUESTIONS ABOUT DEBT AND CREDIT

We owe money to several creditors and are having trouble deciding which to pay first—we just can't pay them all. Do you think a bill consolidation loan would help our situation?

Consolidation loans are tempting because you are able to pay off your creditors with the loan and then make only one payment instead of several. The problem is that a consolidation loan may treat the "symptoms" for a while, but unless a disciplined and diligent lifestyle is adopted, even greater bondage can be created because past habits are not corrected. The result is owing several creditors again, plus having to pay the consolidation loan.

Consolidation loans should never be the first step in resolving a debt problem—instead, budget and discipline. Begin by paying off the highest interest debts first. If all are at a high rate, pay off the ones with the smallest balance. A lower interest consolidation loan might be a possibility but only after a workable budget has been firmly established.

According to the Bible, am I not released from my debts after six years?

In Deuteronomy 15:1-2 there is an admonition not to lend money for a period of more than six years, but that does not apply to those who borrow. If you borrow, you must repay.

I fully pay my credit card bills each month and have no debts other than my home mortgage, but my brother says that Christians should not use credit cards at all. Is he right?

Proverbs 22:3 says, "The prudent sees the evil and hides himself, but the naive go on, and are punished for

it." Credit and credit cards are not
the problem; it is the misuse of credit
that creates the problems. There are
some simple rules for using credit
cards: (1) never use your credit cards
for anything except budgeted purchase; (2) pay your credit cards off
every month; (3) the first month you
have a credit card bill that you cannot pay, destroy the card and never
use it again; (4) finally, keep in mind
that just because you can afford something you don't necessarily need it.

*My bank offers an "overdraft pro-
tection" feature that includes a line of
credit. Wouldn't it be wise to take this
option and save money by avoiding
overdraft charges?*

I've counseled too many couples
who have abused that type of system
to believe it's a good idea. It encourages people not to keep their checking
accounts balanced, and it encourages
them to use credit when they should
really be disciplining themselves. Although some people may make wise
use of this feature, most need to dis-
tance themselves from easy credit.

*I've resolved to get out of debt and
am paying off my creditors as best I
can, but I know my past financial
problems make me a poor credit risk.
How can I regain a good credit rating?*

The difficulty you are experiencing in regaining credit reinforces an important truth taught in Proverbs 22:1: "A good name is to be more desired than great riches, favor is better than silver and gold." It takes a long time to build up a good reputation but little to destroy it. If you have already contacted your creditors personally and asked them to review the credit rating they gave to the credit bureau, there is little else you can do. Although God is faithful to forgive us when we ask forgiveness for violating His principles of finance, that does not mean we can avoid the consequences of our actions. There is no quick fix to bad credit.

Unless you can prove to the credit bureau through canceled checks and receipts that your creditors have misrepresented your credit history, the only way to salvage your name is through disciplined use of whatever remaining credit you have over a long period of time.

Our son is going off to college next fall. Since the school is several hundred miles away, would it be a good idea to give him a credit card to use to travel home and for emergencies?

Proverbs 22:6 says, "Train up a child in the way he should go, even when he is old he will not depart from it." Putting a credit card into the hands of a young person who has not been properly trained in money management and who has not displayed the ability to handle its use over an extended period of time is definitely not a good idea. Even worse, the false security provided by "easy money" through credit often translates into undisciplined spending habits later in life.

On the other hand, children who have been taught the basic principles of money management early and have proved their ability to use them wisely could be trusted to handle a card with no problem. It's up to you to evaluate your son using these criteria.

I am working with a financial counselor to set up a plan to pay off my creditors, but I am still being hounded by collection agencies. Is there any way to get these guys off my case?

The Consumer Protection Act of 1986 gives a measure of relief from harassment by unscrupulous collection agents. Calls late at night or early in the morning are prohibited as well as calls to your place of employment if you have notified the agency that your employer disapproves. A collection agent may not misrepresent himself, provide false information, or threaten legal action when none is intended. If you believe an agent or agency is in violation of this act, contact the Federal Trade Commission in Washington, D.C., for further information.

My husband is the owner of a small business. Due to the economy in our area, we have suffered terrific losses, and the business owes a lot of money. We have been counseled to file for bankruptcy. Is that right?

Psalm 37:21 says, "The wicked borrows and does not pay back, but the righteous is gracious and gives." I do not believe God's Word distinguishes between a personal debt and a business debt. When you borrow money for any purpose, you make a vow or promise to repay what you borrowed. In the short run, you may have to live a frugal life and it may not seem "fair," but in the long run you will have obeyed God, and that is all that will be important one hundred years from now.

Again, that is not to say that you should not seek court protection until you are able to set up a repayment plan. But that is an individual decision between you and the Lord.

Why should I try to be debt-free when my home mortgage carries a low six-percent interest rate and I can make almost twice that by keeping my mortgage and investing my money elsewhere?

I believe everyone should own his home debt-free. If I had to choose to either invest my money and earn ten percent, or to pay off a six percent mortgage, I would pay off the mortgage. Who knows what might happen in the economy that could destroy your investments? What you own belongs to you, and nobody can take it from you.

On a related subject, I've heard the argument that it's illogical to pay off your home because you lose the interest from tax write-offs. That really doesn't make much sense. Let's assume you're in a 30 percent tax bracket right now. If you pay $1,000 in interest, you'll get back approximately $300 in refunded tax. What happened to the other $700? That's not such a good deal. Anytime you pay interest, you lose.

Does the Bible prohibit a Christian from borrowing money from a non-Christian?

God's Word simply says that whatever is borrowed must be repaid. It doesn't specify whether a believer should borrow from another believer or from a nonbeliever. It doesn't make any difference as far as repayment is concerned. Proverbs 22:7 cautions us that a lender becomes an authority over a borrower.

APPROACHING FINANCIAL FREEDOM

ACKNOWLEDGE GOD'S OWNERSHIP DAILY

Be certain that the affairs and decisions of each day are surrendered to God. Since problems are day-by-day occurrences, our acknowledgment of God's authority and forgiveness should be daily as well. Each day must begin with a clean heart, meaning that we have no unconfessed sin in our lives.

What are the essential elements in making sound financial decisions? Adequate knowledge and the wisdom to apply it. "The fear of the Lord is the beginning of knowledge; fools despise wisdom and instruction" (Proverbs 1:7). Thus it is vital to recognize that you are seeking God's knowledge and wisdom when you seek financial freedom.

To do so you must surrender every decision to God. "So you will find favor and good repute in the sight of

God and man. Trust in the Lord with all your heart, and do not lean on your own understanding. In all your ways acknowledge Him, and He will make your paths straight" (Proverbs 3:4-6).

ACCEPT GOD'S DIRECTION

Once you have surrendered control of your finances to God, accept His judgment. Do not precondition your response by expecting only increases. Paul said he had learned to be abased and to abound but in all things to give thanks. After you have surrendered decision-making to God, accept His wisdom.

God may be using your adversities as a testimony for other people or to reinforce a lesson. I have found it to be true in my own life that during times of trial we grow the most.

Don't seek escape from difficulties; seek peace during them. "Be anxious for nothing, but in everything by prayer and supplication with thanksgiving let your requests be made known to God" (Philippians 4:6). In every decision trust God to guide you. Verify your decisions by checking them against the Lord's Word, confirming them in prayer, and accepting His answer.

There is one final step in accepting God's direction: "In everything give thanks; for this is God's will for you in Christ Jesus" (1 Thessalonians 5:18). When you ask God for a decision and He answers, thank Him, whether or not it is the answer you were seeking.

I once counseled a couple who were having financial difficulties. Their income was not sufficient to meet their wants, and they had drifted into financial bondage. In reviewing the circumstances with the husband, I found that he was not really satisfied in his work. It seemed that his company was not dealing fairly with him because of his Christian commitment. That hindered his witness in dealing with customers. I asked him if he was committed to seeking God's wisdom rather than man's. He replied, "Yes, I am." I then asked if he was willing to surrender the decision about his employment to God and let Him decide the next step. After we prayed about it, he reaffirmed his commitment to God's will no matter what it was.

He prayed for two things: that God would provide a definite direction concerning his work and that He would relieve him of his debt. God worked specifically on both.

First, he was convicted to confront his employers concerning their attitude about his religious beliefs. They declared they no longer had a place for him in their company and dismissed him. Upon termination, they surrendered the money that was due him in a savings plan. That money was sufficient to pay off all his debts.

Although it was not the method he would have chosen, he thanked God for the answer.

Christians should learn to accept God's wisdom when they ask for it. God loves us deeply, and He will never give us less than His best.

ESTABLISH THE TITHE

Give God the first part of your income as a testimony of His ownership. "Give, and it will be given to you; good measure, pressed down, shaken together, running over, they will pour into your lap. For by your standard of measure it will be measured to you in return" (Luke 6:38). This is an essential step to financial freedom.

The tithe is a spiritual investment and cannot be evaluated on the
basis of profit and loss. Many Christians look at tithing in worldly terms,
but God is the only business manager
who can make 90 percent go farther
than 100 percent.

SACRIFICE

The concept of sacrifice is not
popular with most Christians. Most
of us like to discuss this subject in
generalities rather than specifics. It's
all right for the pastor to mention
sacrifice when he talks about mis-
sionaries or "full-time" Christians,
but when he talks about giving up
golf or a new car for God's work, sud-
denly he becomes a radical.

Those who have truly surrendered
their finances to God also experience
His faithfulness. "And everyone who
has left houses or brothers or sisters
or father or mother or children or
farms for My name's sake, shall receive many times as much, and shall
inherit eternal life" (Matthew 19:29).

God provides many opportuni-
ties to invest in the lives of others in
need. Thus, if a Christian wants to
give God control of his finances, he
must

1. daily surrender to God every financial decision, no matter how large or small;
2. accept God's wisdom for every decision;
3. give at least a tithe to God as testimony of His ownership;
4. willingly seek to share with other people, even if it requires sacrifice.

PRINCIPLES OF FINANCIAL DECISION-MAKING

These principles for financial decisions summarize how God would have us manage money.

AVOID SPECULATION

Every Christian should seek God's increase and make no provision for speculative schemes. Many times enticing programs are not only unethical but border on being illegal—for example, pyramid franchising systems, multilevel marketing systems, unregistered stock offers, and scores of other questionable ventures.

Assess every "opportunity" in relation to your own commitment to Christ. Do not let others make your financial decisions for you. Make your decisions in light of your goals; evaluate whether a venture is necessary.

Often in speculative schemes you will lose your witness, your credibility, and your money. So avoid them. Money that has taken years to save can be lost in an instant.

The temptation of easy money and the emotionalism of its sponsors will sorely test your commitment. Satan doesn't have to attack in a "spiritual" area if he gets a foothold in your finances, because that will soon affect you spiritually. *Sound Investments* explains more details of typical get-rich-quick schemes.

KEEP YOUR FINANCES CURRENT

The second principle of financial decision-making is to manage your finances on a current basis. In other words, make no allowance in your financial planning to borrow money beyond your ability to repay, even for one day. Many people become involved in investment programs they cannot afford and borrow money to invest where repayment is dependent on a future event. To do so is to flirt with financial disaster.

If what you buy jeopardizes your financial freedom, forget it. Impulse-buying, either for investment or consumption, is disastrous. When you evaluate a purchase, consider the obligation in light of your known income.

Certainly that is a conservative attitude, but that philosophy is directed toward long-range peace, not short-range profit. "For which one of you, when he wants to build a tower, does not first sit down and calculate the cost, to see if he has enough to complete it? Otherwise, when he has laid a foundation, and is not able to finish, all who observe it begin to ridicule him, saying, 'This man began to build and was not able to finish'" (Luke 14:28-30). Make your plans in light of present circumstances, not a future event.

Maintain the principle of staying debt-free; make every decision on the basis of whether it may ultimately result in bondage.

CONSIDER YOUR WITNESS

Consider every decision on the basis of its effect on the work and reputation of Christ. Do not put God in a financial corner and place Him in the role of "bailer." We are told in 1 Corinthians 10:31, "Whether, then, you eat or drink or whatever you do, do all to the glory of God."

To launch out on feelings (even to do God's work) and then depend on God to bail you out is not according to His plan. Christians in full-time ministry should accept this as a basic financial principle. If one must borrow beyond God's people to do His work, beware! "The rich rules over the poor, and the borrower becomes the lender's slave" (Proverbs 22:7).

God will not frustrate His work for lack of money; neither will He place a Christian organization in servitude to a secular institution.

This principle also applies to dealing unethically with others. There are no small lies or small thefts, only liars and thieves.

If you deal unfairly or unethically with someone, your witness will suffer. Establish that no matter what the circumstance, you will tell the whole truth to the best of your ability. If you stumble, make restitution and admit your error. God will honor your commitment.

GIVE TO THE NEEDS OF OTHERS

Avoid lending to a person in need if it is possible to give. Why? The witness and fellowship of giving is lasting whereas the temporary gratitude of a loan quickly fades.

I recall reading an article in which the question was asked: "What is a distant relative?" The answer: "It is a close relative you loan money to." What is a distant Christian friend? It is a close Christian friend to whom you loan money.

If someone approaches you for financial help to acquire his wants or desires, you should question whether to supply anything at all. But if he or she is in need and on your heart, you have a responsibility from God to supply that need.

NEVER COSIGN

Cosigning means to pledge your assets against the debts of someone else. Scripture specifically forbids this when it speaks of "surety" or "striking of hands." There are many references to this in Proverbs.

Note that Solomon, king and ruler of Israel, wrote much about avoiding cosigning. It seems obvious that time after time lenders came before him collecting cosigned debts, taking every possession from those who cosigned. He noted how ridiculous that was, saying, "Friend, they will not only take your house, they'll take your bed with it."

This warning goes beyond personal cosigning. It also applies to business (with the possible exception of a privately held business). If you work for a company and consistently cosign notes, you are also violating this principle.

"My son, if you have become surety for your neighbor, have given a pledge for a stranger, if you have been snared with the words of your mouth, have been caught with the words of your mouth, do this then, my son, and deliver yourself; since you have come into the hand of your neighbor, go, humble yourself, and importune your neighbor" (Proverbs 6:1-3).

Of all the areas of Scripture, this would seem to be one of the most explicit. Yet, we continually violate this principle and rationalize it away with human logic. Ask any banker what type of loans he considers the most likely to default, and practically everyone will say cosigned notes. Not only is cosigning a violation of the principle of surety, but by doing so, the cosigner may be interfering with God's plan for someone else.

AVOID INDULGENCE

Discern the difference between needs, wants, and desires in every purchase. That applies not only to purchases of material goods but to investments as well. Before you invest, ask why you are investing. Is it to help you fulfill a need? Is it to help you further God's work? Or is it to satisfy a hungry ego?

If you believe the purchase is within God's will, you will have peace. But if you assess that the purchase is a desire or a whim, stop to check God's principles. Many Christians are frustrated because they cannot distinguish between luxuries and necessities. Consequently, they seek fulfillment through the same channels as non-Christians and then wonder why they have a fruitless Christian walk. I believe God wants us to live comfortably. But He does not want us to live lavishly.

At a time when our resources could be used to promote God's work throughout the world, we should evaluate every financial motive. "Do not love the world, nor the things in the world. If any one loves the world, the love of the Father is not in him. For all that is in the world, the lust of the flesh and the lust of the eyes and the boastful pride of life, is not from the Father, but is from the world" (1 John 2:15-16).

PREPARE FOR DECREASES

Being prepared for unexpected decreases in funds is a vital part of wise decision-making. When you make a financial decision, consider what would happen if you had even a small decrease in funds.

This is especially important when the wife works and expenses are incurred on the assumption that two incomes are guaranteed. What if you are forced to reduce your income? What if God asks you to do something in His work that requires a reduced income? To the Christian who is totally trusting in Christ, the quality of life is independent of the circumstances, as Paul states in Philippians 4:12-13: "I know how to get along with humble means, and I also know how to live in prosperity; in any and every circumstance I have learned the secret of being filled and going hungry, both of having abundance and suffering need. I can do all things through Him who strengthens me."

Do not operate at the upper limit of your income; instead make financial decisions considering that you may need to reduce your standard of living. The ability to thank God in every circumstance demonstrates full dependence and trust in Him.

IF YOU DON'T HAVE PEACE, DON'T BUY

Often we are not responsive enough to God's Word or presence to hear Him except through that inner turmoil known as a lack of peace. As a last resort, God will use this to provide direction. Accordingly, if you do not have peace, do not get involved. If a quick decision is required, do not get involved. Take the time to think and pray about it; perhaps God has an alternative provision for you.

Many times I have made decisions on the spur of the moment. Seldom have I not regretted those decisions later. Determine that you will not make a decision under pressure. You may miss a few "good deals," but you will also miss a great many bad ones. "It is the blessing of the Lord that makes rich, and He adds no sorrow to it" (Proverbs 10:22).

Become sensitive to God's inner guidance; He will always provide direction if you seek it. Even when we fail to see the right path clearly in God's Word or hear it in prayer, God will place unrest inside that will keep us from financial bondage.

Bankruptcy

The term *bankruptcy* comes from two Latin words meaning "bench" and "break"; thus, its literal meaning is "broken bench." Under Roman law, after gathering together and dividing up the assets of a delinquent debtor, the creditors would break the debtor's workbench as a punishment and a warning to other indebted tradesmen. Bankrupt individuals were regarded as thieves who deserved severe penalty. Romans deprived them of their civil rights, and many other societies stigmatized them by requiring that they dress in a particular identifying garb.

In our society revisions to the bankruptcy laws and changes in consumer attitudes toward bankruptcy have fostered a climate in which people regard bankruptcy as a more plausible remedy for financial problems than they once did.

In 1978 there were about 50,000 personal bankruptcies in our country. In 1988 there were nearly 500,000 personal bankruptcies in America, according to an article in *U.S.A. Today*. Assuming this trend continues, we can realistically expect to see a million bankruptcies each year by the year 2000!

Those statistics spell great difficulty for many small merchants and for the credit industry as a whole. But even worse, they reflect a decline in the responsibility index for the average American family, both Christian and non-Christian alike.

A revised bankruptcy code enacted in 1978 (the Bankruptcy Act of 1978) took effect on October 1, 1979. The code consolidated some chapters of previous law pertaining to business reorganization and sought to streamline the administration of the bankruptcy courts, but its most sweeping changes involved personal bankruptcy. The revision made bankruptcy an attractive option to troubled debtors, especially because it increased the amount of assets that could be exempt from liquidation.

About half of the personal bankruptcies in this country are taken by young couples who have charged and borrowed far beyond their abilities to pay. They see bankruptcy as their only release from the financial bondage that threatens their marriage and sometimes their health.

In a recent counseling session a couple revealed that they owed $6,000 in credit card bills, $11,000 for a consolidation loan, and $15,000 for a family loan to buy a home. "Obviously," the husband said, "another consolidation loan won't help. The only thing that will help us is a fresh start." A friend in their church had offered to lend them the money to file for bankruptcy. They came for counsel because a wise pastor knew that bankruptcy would be just another quick fix. A review of their financial history convinced them that history would repeat itself if they didn't change their habits.

It's amazing that the average family filing for bankruptcy only owes about $4,000. The problem is that it's usually many small bills, and most of them are delinquent. They may have the capacity to pay their creditors, but that would require at least two years of financial sacrifice. We are a generation of quick-fix addicts, and personal responsibility has not been taught for a long time, even within Christianity.

IS BANKRUPTCY SCRIPTURAL?

This is not a simple question to answer. God's Word clearly says that a believer should be responsible for his promises and repay what he owes. "When you make a vow to God, do not be late in paying it, for He takes no delight in fools. Pay what you vow! It is better that you should not vow than that you should vow and not pay" (Ecclesiastes 5:4-5). Does that mean that in the interim you should not take the legal remedy of court protection until you have the ability to repay? Often that is an individual decision. First and foremost, a Christian must be willing to accept the absolute requirement to repay everyone he or she owes.

The issue of motive must also be addressed. Is bankruptcy being declared to protect the legitimate rights of the creditors? The answer to this question can be found in whether or not assets are purposely withheld from the creditors. For example, many times when someone files for corporate or personal bankruptcy protection, assets are transferred to the spouse or other family members. So if the intent is merely to protect the assets of the debtor, without due consideration of the creditors, the action is unscriptural. It would be better to suffer the loss of all assets rather than lose one's integrity. Proverbs 3:27-28 says, "Do not withhold good from those to whom it is due, when it is in your power to do it. Do not say to your neighbor, 'Go, and come back, and tomorrow I will give it,' when you have it with you."

Bankruptcy is a serious matter, and at best both sides lose. The creditors lose much of the money they are owed, and the debtors lose much of the respect they previously had. There is still stigma associated with bankruptcy, and until the last creditor is repaid it will remain. However, a person who has filed for bankruptcy can turn a negative situation into a positive one by making a commitment to repay what is legitimately owed. Once that commitment is made, the individual should look to God to provide the means to do so.

THE YEAR OF REMISSION OR JUBILEE

One counselee told me that bankruptcy was a biblical principle based upon the year of remission discussed in Deuteronomy 15:1-2. According to God's Word, there was to be a release of debtors every seventh year. However, this was a directive for God's children and was always an option of the lender, not the borrower.

The year of jubilee, as discussed in Leviticus 25:10, was literally the seventh year of remission. Again, it was the responsibility and option of the lender, not the borrower, to release debts.

BANKRUPTCY IS A SPIRITUAL INDICATOR

God's Word teaches that the way we handle our money is the clearest reflection of our spiritual value system. Excessive debts, even bankruptcies, are not our real problems—they are external indicators of internal problems. Literally, they reflect a person's attitude. That is not to indict those who are in debt or file for bankruptcy, but it reflects what Christ said: "He who is faithful in a very little thing is faithful also in much; and he who is unrighteous in a very little thing is unrighteous also in much. If therefore you have not been faithful in the use of unrighteous mammon, who will entrust the true riches to you?" (Luke 16:10-11).

I recently received a call from a pastor who was considering filing for bankruptcy because of a heavy debt. He was fearful of his creditors obtaining judgments or even garnishments against him. "It's not fair that they can attach my salary," he said. "I won't be able to feed my family." I asked him if they had tricked him into borrowing their money. They had not. I asked him to put himself in the place of the lender. If that lender were in his congregation, would he respond to a salvation message delivered by a pastor who had bankrupted to avoid paying a debt? Then I asked him to consider what Christ would do if He were in his position. After all, isn't that what we're instructed to do as Christ's followers? We are to do nothing solely for our own benefit. "Do not merely look out for your own personal interests, but also for the interests of others" (Philippians 2:4). We are to be imitators of Christ (cf. Ephesians 5:1).

The pastor stood up to his burden, asked for the forgiveness of his creditors, and cut up all his credit cards. He confessed his error before his church and found several kindred spirits in the congregation. There was some wagging of tongues to be sure, but in great part there was healing and understanding.

REPAYMENT IS A VOW

A principle that has been greatly overlooked in our generation is that of making a vow. A vow is literally a promise. When someone borrows money, he makes a promise to repay according to the agreed-upon conditions of the loan. Once an agreement is reached, repayment is not an option; it's an absolute as far as God is concerned. The rights all fall to the lender, and the borrower literally becomes the lender's servant.

As representatives of Jesus Christ to the world, Christians are admonished to think ahead and consider the consequences of their actions. That's why Scripture teaches so many principles of borrowing, lending, and especially the misuse of credit. But once a Christian borrows, he's made a vow to repay. "When you make a vow to God, do not be late in paying it, for He takes no delight in fools. Pay what you vow! It is better that you should not vow than that you should vow and not pay" (Ecclesiastes 5:4-5).

WHAT ABOUT INVOLUNTARY BANKRUPTCY?

I was working with a young couple who had accumulated nearly $40,000 in business debts before they closed their doors. They were being hounded by creditors on every side. They had sold their home, one car, and virtually every asset to reduce the debt from about $60,000. They didn't want to go bankrupt and tried to negotiate a repayment schedule with their creditors but to no avail. Creditor after creditor filed judgments against them. The bottom line was that virtually every creditor told them to file bankruptcy and get it over with. They told the husband they wouldn't work with him because he had no assets and that they would rather write off the debts through bankruptcy.

My counsel was that he was not responsible for what the creditors did or didn't do. He was responsible before God for his actions. I recommended that he respond literally according to Proverbs 6:2-3. He should humble himself before his creditors and ask them to work with him.

They, unfortunately, refused and forced him into involuntary bankruptcy. Once they filed bankruptcy against him, he was legally but not scripturally released from the debts. He has diligently worked ever since to pay off the debts one at a time and will continue to do so.

A counselee once asked, "Would God direct someone to go bankrupt?" My answer was, "I don't see how, since that would refute His own Word." God's Word says a wicked man borrows but does not repay (Psalm 37:21). God desires that we be righteous, not wicked.

"But will God forgive me if I go bankrupt?" he asked. God says He will forgive any sin, past, present, and future, if we confess it. Bankruptcy is a legal remedy, not a scriptural remedy. It is understandable that under the pressures of excessive debts a Christian would yield to a quick-fix, but it doesn't make bankruptcy any more scriptural.

Involuntary bankruptcy can be initiated by several creditors who wish to attach all available assets and force an individual or corporation to liquidate. A good biblical case can be made for the position that since the creditors initiated the action, they have settled any and all claims. But in our society this action is often necessary to preempt a debtor from liquidating all assets and spending the money. A Christian's obligation is to repay according to the original terms. "Do not withhold good from those to whom it is due, when it is in your power to do it" (Proverbs 3:27).

CORPORATE BANKRUPTCY

Corporate bankruptcy laws and procedures are much too complicated to cover in this booklet. Therefore, only a simple overview is presented here to help show the basic differences among the various "chapters" of the bankruptcy code. Specific advice should be sought from a qualified attorney.

CHAPTER 11

This section details how a corporation may file for federal bankruptcy protection and continue to operate while working out a plan to repay its creditors. Normally a corporation has three years to repay creditors at least the amount that a liquidation of the assets under chapter 7 of the code would have provided. Otherwise, the corporation may face the possibility of total dissolution under the provisions of a chapter 7 (straight) bankruptcy.

CHAPTER 7

If the bankruptcy judge does not believe a company can realistically become viable, he can decide to dissolve the company under chapter 7 of the code. The company is carefully inventoried and, under the supervision of a bankruptcy trustee appointed by the court, dissolved and the assets sold off to satisfy the creditors. In most instances the creditors will receive only a percentage of the original outstanding debts.

PERSONAL BANKRUPTCY

CHAPTER 13

This action is the individual equivalent of a chapter 11 bankruptcy for a corporation. It is intended to allow an individual (or couple) to operate under court protection from their creditors for about three (sometimes up to five) years. As with a corporation, these individuals must be able to show that a reasonable percentage of their debts can be paid during the specified period.

There are specific limits placed on the amount of debt allowed and on the amount of assets necessary to qualify an individual to file for bankruptcy protection under chapter 13. The court usually requires a frequent accounting and review of the finances to ensure that the conditions of the plan are being met.

If the individual faithfully fulfills his obligations under the chapter 13 plan for the full period of time specified, the judge will formally discharge (forgive) any remaining balance due on all dischargeable debts. Examples of these types of debts are discussed under chapter 7 below.

CHAPTER 7

This is a plan for personal financial dissolution. As with a corporate chapter 7 bankruptcy, an individual's property is inventoried and liquidated to satisfy the creditors. Specified items, monies, and personal effects are exempt from this process. Under this plan a trustee is appointed to oversee the liquidation. If it has been determined that the individual has not withheld any nonexempt assets and has been honest in his dealings with his creditors and the trustee, the judge will grant a discharge—the formal forgiveness of all remaining debt.

It is important to realize that debts are placed into two categories—dischargeable and non-dischargeable debts. Dischargeable debts can be forgiven. They include such debts as rent, credit card bills, and medical bills. Non-dischargeable debts must be repaid and include student loans, alimony, and taxes.

Debts are also categorized as secured and unsecured. Secured debts (i.e., those for which the item is pledged as security—in writing—if the loan is not repaid) are usually dischargeable, but the item pledged must be returned or paid for. However, if other property that was already owned is pledged as security, that property may be retained. Unsecured debts, which are almost always dischargeable, include personal loans from friends or relatives and credit card accounts.

FARM REORGANIZATION

Farmers have historically been treated differently from other debtors under the bankruptcy code. In the 1930s and 40s farmers were given special consideration under section 75 of the Bankruptcy Act, known as the Frazier-Lemke Act of 1933, which stipulates that a farmer cannot be the subject of an involuntary petition (creditor-initiated dissolution). Farmers' special status was broadened even more with the passage of chapter 12 of the 1986 Bankruptcy Act. Prior to chapter 12, chapter 11 relief was the principal method of reorganization utilized by farmers.

As may be deduced by its position in the Bankruptcy Code, chapter 12 contains some elements of chapter 11 and some of chapter 13. Chapter 12 is limited to individuals (and sometimes corporations or partnerships) engaged in farming enterprises, with debts totaling no more than $1.5 million and sufficient annual income to make payments under a chapter 12 plan.

In a chapter 12 case a trustee is automatically appointed as in a chapter 13 case, but the debtor continues as a "debtor-in-possession" and has similar powers as a trustee serving in a chapter 11 case. The farmer may choose to convert his chapter 12 case to a chapter 7. Other unique particulars of a chapter 12 bankruptcy may be obtained from a qualified attorney.

FILING FOR BANKRUPTCY

Filing a chapter 13 bankruptcy plan is a relatively simple procedure when compared to filing for protection under the other chapters, so a general description of filing for a chapter 13 plan is presented here. However, an attorney should be consulted prior to filing under any chapter, especially for those other than chapter 13.

In order to file for bankruptcy under chapter 13, forms must be completed showing the debtor's monthly income, ordinary living expenses, and the difference, which could be applied toward the debts. Filling out and filing these forms (along with the applicable filing fee) stops all creditor collection efforts. Arrangements can then be made to stop any wage attachments or automatic debt payment deductions. Under chapter 13 all payments to creditors are made through a court-appointed trustee.

Approximately one month after the initial filing, the debtor meets the trustee at the courthouse to discuss various aspects of the plan, outstanding debts, and property. Once the plan is confirmed by a bankruptcy judge, it immediately goes into operation. The debtor pays the trustee the amount specified by the plan each month, and the trustee pays the bills and deals with all creditors.

At the end of about three years the debtor and trustee appear again before the bankruptcy judge. If the plan has been followed faithfully, the judge will formally discharge any remaining dischargeable debts.

ANSWERS TO QUESTIONS ABOUT BANKRUPTCY

If I file for bankruptcy protection, what happens to debts cosigned by friends or relatives?

Any cosigners are still liable to pay whatever portion of the debt remains unpaid.

Can I avoid the IRS through a bankruptcy?

Many people have the mistaken impression that filing for bankruptcy voids an obligation to the IRS. Not so. The bankruptcy code excludes several categories of debt from the set-aside provisions of the law (non-dischargeable debts); these non-dischargeable debts include federal and state income tax liabilities and federally backed school loans.

Should I file for bankruptcy because of a large lawsuit judgment?

It is not impossible or even unlikely to be sued for millions of dollars over an accident in our society. So it is prudent for individuals to carry appropriate liability insurance. However, in the face of an unreasonable judgment in which damages are clearly punitive rather than compensatory, filing for protection may be an option to prayerfully consider. Refer to *Insurance Plans* for suggestions on appropriate insurance coverage.

What is the difference between a "straight" bankruptcy and a chapter 13 plan?

Straight bankruptcy (chapter 7) is a legal way to make most debts disappear with no legal requirement to repay them. A chapter 13 plan provides a means for repaying most, if not all, debts under court supervision and protection.

What will chapter 13 repayment proceedings do to my credit rating?

Credit reporting agencies are allowed to keep a notation of chapter 13 proceedings on file for ten years. The notes include the total amount of debts owed and the amount actually repaid under chapter 13.

Will I lose my job if I go through bankruptcy?

Employers are forbidden to fire an employee because of bankruptcy proceedings. However, certain jobs in which the employee must be bonded (such as a jewelry clerk or bank teller) may be jeopardized.